W. Lehmbruck

AUGUST HOFF

WILHELM LEHMBRUCK

LIFE AND WORK

PALL MALL PRESS · LONDON

First published in Great Britain in 1969
by Pall Mall Press, Ltd.,
5 Cromwell Place, London S.W. 7

English translation copyright 1969 in New York
by Frederick A. Praeger, Inc., New York

SBN 269 67130 7

Printed in Germany

To the memory of

FRAU ANITA LEHMBRUCK

AUTHOR'S NOTE

This study of Wilhelm Lehmbruck was first published in 1936, and immediately ran afoul of the German censorship, which objected to the jacket illustration because of its symbolic content. A year later, Lehmbruck was relegated to the ranks of degenerate artists. Nonetheless the book sold out. Howewer, permission for a second edition was not granted.

Soon after the collapse of the Nazi regime the publisher wished to prepare a new edition, but a variety of factors delayed this plan for some years, until 1961 when the second German edition appeared.

I am indebted to the late Frau Anita Lehmbruck, widow of the artist, and to her son Guido for making available to me much background material and information, and I am grateful to the Rembrandt Verlag for providing me with the opportunity to expand and supplement the original edition.

August Hoff.

Tired Warrior. Pen and Ink

LEHMBRUCK'S MISSION

'Sculpture is the essence of things, the essence of nature, that which is eternally human.' Thus wrote Wilhelm Lehmbruck. The eternally human is man's soul, and Lehmbruck's sculptures speak the language of the soul. The figures he created expressed the essence of man. Their immanent life is their essential being. His sculptures are animated as sculpture had not been for many years, and neither his contemporaries nor those who came after him have rivaled him.

Hidden under the surface lies the true substance, the inner experience, and it is veiled by an unfathomable secret. Here a pure and gentle soul, a heroic figure filled with the sorrow and joy of this inner vision, is given expression, ennobled by the grandeur of the ultimate truth. Reverent and still, thoughtful and dedicated, his figures listen to profound, seldom-heard voices. Lehmbruck's figures were shaped by inspiration, intuition, instinct, and deep feeling. He did not arrive at his conception via intellectual deliberation.

Lehmbruck's sculptures are completely free from all trace of fussiness. Everything has become internalized. Stillness and serenity is the keynote of their form, and the keynote of their inner meaning is meditation and longing, dreams and sadness, doubt and brooding. Their every detail pulsates with deep emotion and becomes the yardstick for the entire work. Lehmbruck himself said: The detail is the gauge of the whole.

To say that which cannot be said, to make the impenetrable visible, Lehmbruck had to disassemble the body and reconstruct it as a new spiritual reality. The essence of truly creative art here stands revealed.

9

Lehmbruck's figures, though never schematic, become the symbol, the true mark of man's inner life. One remains aware of his unrivaled masterful command of nature, of a highly sensitive, sensual pleasure in the beauty and nobility of the human body. The new form endeavors to achieve an architectural quality, a purity of structure. Given this creative principle, one might speak of an inner, not a derivative, relationship with the Gothic. The bodies, growing out of the earthly realm, reach up into metaphysical heights. In this striving and climbing, in this longing and dedication to something higher, in this ultimately spiritual aspect, lies Lehmbruck's secret Gothic. All of his works, despite the bold rhythm of his figures, their austere simplicity, the ruggedness of their surfaces, the simplicity of line, are surrounded by an aura of harmonious and innate nobility. By seeming to sacrifice external beauty, he has managed to endow them with greater inner beauty. Because Lehmbruck carried within himself a compelling longing for true beauty and perfection, one can, in discussing his style, speak with equal justification of secret Classicism.

The creations of Wilhelm Lehmbruck are the testaments of a brooding spirit. It was not given to him to complete a work happily, while still intoxicated with the excitement of creativity. He approached the problems with circumspection, nursing the idea for a long time, letting it mature, working endlessly on his figures to achieve ultimate perfection. His hands and his mind continued to experiment with and work on figures long since completed and exhibited. He was wont to cast separately parts of a big work which seemed to him particularly successful, as for example the head or torso of a sculpture. For him, the head probably expressed the spiritual content of the work, while the torso, stripped of the melodic accompaniment of the arms, represented the sought-after sculptural structure. Thus he substituted the part for the whole. He imparted a completely new meaning to the torso as the essence of the sculptural intention. This was the mark of a spirit in

10

search of the ultimate answer, of perfection free from arbitrariness and decorative embellishment. Because of this search for perfection, and despite the wealth of ideas, attested to by numerous drawings and prints, his total output remained comparatively small.

Many of his drawings and etchings have a joyous airiness and lightness, a fresh immediacy of inspiration, a sure feeling for the values represented by line and plane. His sculptures, on the other hand, strike one as somewhat weighed down and pain-wracked. They give evidence of the bitter, profound struggle raging in the breast of the artist,

The Fallen. Charcoal

a lonely, withdrawn man given to contemplation, brooding, and doubt. He sought to find the way back to unity and oneness through his work. His 'Ascendant Youth' and 'Head of a Thinker' seem like spiritual self-portraits. Every truly creative act is daring, and it becomes doubly burdened by responsibility in the case of an artist with ambitious goals, a trailblazer seeking new approaches. The life of such a man must perforce become hard and problematical. Creative effort is a heroic business.

BACKGROUND AND EDUCATION

Gifted men frequently come of simple stock. Wilhelm Lehmbruck, a miner's son born on January 4 1881, in Duisburg, was the fourth of eight children. Duisburg was a town with mines and a growing industry, but on the whole it was rural in character. Lehmbruck's ancestors were peasants from Gahlen, a village of the Lower Rhine region near Westphalia. His teachers described him as a quiet, introspective youngster, and that is the impression he gives in a portrait painted in 1903 by one of his fellow students at the art school, the painter H. Wettig (p. 153). Holding a book, the twenty-two-year old Lehmbruck, leaning forward slightly, sits with tightly-closed lips and a serious, brooding expression, mature far beyond his years.

In appearance and habits Wilhelm Lehmbruck resembled his father. But it was his mother who supported him in his ambition to become an artist. The unusual talent of the boy manifested itself at a surprisingly early age. Without any help from anyone, he began to whittle figures with his penknife out of chalk or plaster fragments for his teachers and relatives. He carved out of the block without making models. He would translate the one-dimensional, simple pictures of his school books into spatial values—statues of Charlemagne and Luther, of medieval knights and angels. The remarkable feature of these early efforts was his instinctive grasp of the structural values of monuments he had never even seen but knew only from pictures. The fourteen-year-old was understandably proud of one of his models, a small-scale rendering of a statue of Frederick-William, the Great Elector, and he submitted it with his application for entry to an art-school in Düsseldorf.

13

Lehmbruck entered the school in the spring of 1895, and during the next four years he sought to learn everything being taught there. In the course of his studies he became convinced that the fine arts were what he wanted, but since his family was not able to support him—his father had died in 1899—he had to find ways of supporting himself. He did this by making designs for industrial products and illustrations for scientific books. He also made a bust of Queen Luise after a portrait by Gustav Richter for presentation to the mayor of his home town at a celebration in 1898. In 1905, he made a small bronze copy of the baroque equestrian statue of Johann Wilhelm of the Palatinate in the Town Square of Düsseldorf, for sale as a souvenir. He also did a few sculptures in the then favored sentimental mode, some of which he was able to sell. Then he began to get portrait commissions, and with his earnings he would treat himself to short trips; once he went to neighboring Holland. After finishing at the school in Düsseldorf, he worked as an assistant in a sculptor's studio until 1901, when he was able to enrol in the Art Academy, where he soon became the prize pupil of Karl Janssen. During the six years he spent at the Academy he was given a studio, models, and stipends. Thus he was able to perfect his skill and technique in comparative comfort, free from petty worries and problems.

Given the academicism of his time, it should not come as a surprise that he worked along purely academic lines and that his later personal style was only vaguely hinted at. We are acquainted with his early works largely through pictures, but some are to be found at the Duisburg museum, among them a large charcoal drawing by the sixteen-year-old Lehmbruck. This picture, 'Study of an Old Man with a Skull,' shows Lehmbruck's mastery of anatomy and his remarkably sensitive handling of the graphic medium. Little wonder, then, that he was the pride of his drawing instructor. Among his earliest works at the Academy was a large nude, which he did in 1902. In this, he was concerned primarily with displaying his technical skill and mastery of anatomical details. This was followed by another large work in the same vein, 'The Shot-Putter.' Then there is the 'Siegfried testing his Sword,' possibly a model for a statue. It is a work quite in keeping with the superficial dramatic mode of the time. Even though these were only exercises, they served notice of his intention to apply his enormous talent to works of a large scale. What was still lacking was the inner greatness which alone justifies works of such scope. But everything he did at that time revealed his seriousness of purpose and the power of his creative drive.

The experiences of his early life invariably affect the work of every artist; hence the themes which occupied the young Lehmbruck are not without interest. Lehmbruck did not have to read the naturalist literature of his time to know firsthand the problems of everyday life and society. He, the miner's son, had been familiar with them since his early youth, and they had helped shape his somber view of life. His 'Stone Mover' and his later version of the same figure, the 'Stone Roller' or 'Labor,' are almost like self-portraits, as if he himself were the man pitting his body against the superhuman weight of the block of stone. It is both symbol and premonition of the arduous task lying ahead of him. A mine disaster inspired his 'Mine Gas,' a huge model for a memorial completely in the literary style of the era: a woman throwing herself over a dead miner, next to her an uncomprehending child and a fellow worker bidding his dead comrade farewell. He also did a sensitively formed head of the same woman in marble. Lehmbruck at one time toyed with the idea of doing a monument to labor: a round base with reliefs of workers—a smith, a steelworker, and others—and an allegorical figure of the rewards of labor. His 'Miner' (p. 51) and a foundry worker he did are evidence to his great indebtedness to Meunier, and he was still strongly influenced by Meunier when he did his 'Two Beggars,' 'Rivals,' and 'Temptation' (p. 65). A few years later a fascinating, strong naturalism began to assert itself in his life-

15

size bust 'The Old Woman' and in the blind couple of 'Toward the Goal.' Hand in hand with these serious themes and realistic depictions we find a quest for harmony and beauty, for gracefulness and the ideal man. This longing posed the threat of his falling prey to the conventions of academic classicism and the Salon, a danger which loomed particularly large in works such as 'Grace,' 'Young Love,' and the plaque 'The Road to Beauty.' The fact that these works brought him his greatest success in Düsseldorf is not too surprising, given the then prevalent ideas on art.

Lehmbruck's enormous talent and his fidelity to the ideal of the Academy made him the pride of his teachers. Thus it came about that the Academy, contrary to normal practice, bought a work by one of its prize pupils for its collection, Lehmbruck's early 'Bather' (1905, p. 52). The proceeds from this sale made it possible for Lehmbruck to spend a few months in Italy. His subsequent work reflected the impact of the art he saw there. Later, in 1912, after completing a large marble sculpture for Duisburg, he was again able to go to Italy, but this time he saw it with completely different eyes.

The mysterious relationship of mother and child, their close bond and gentle affection, expressed so movingly by Lehmbruck, was a theme that occupied him in his early years. His first Italian trip seems to have inspired the three versions of that theme which he made in 1907. The full-size bronze in the Folkswang Museum of Essen (pp. 54, 55) depicts the closeness of mother and child by look and gesture, though it only narrates it, without really embodying it. In the high reliefs 'Lost in Thought' (p. 57) and 'Mother and Child,' the formal connection has become more a symbol of human affection. Finally, a very small sculpture, 'Mother Protecting Her Child,' made in his last year in Düsseldorf, should be mentioned. In his maturity, Lehmbruck was again to take up the inexhaustible theme of motherhood (pp. 122, 123).

An observant and sensitive artist, Lehmbruck did not simply re-

Martha. Oil, 1912. Duisburg

produce what he saw; he interpreted it as well. At first, this probing insight did not yet permeate the entire work. The 'Portrait Bust of the Painter W.' (p. 50) is reminiscent of Rodin's portrait sculptures. His portrait of a youth, the marble bust of 'Count St.,' is a gentle and sensitive study.

Lehmbruck's works of his final Düsseldorf years give evidence of his sure feeling for spatial values and for large forms. In addition to some tomb reliefs of a somewhat pre-Raphaelite cast there are the reliefs 'Sorrowing Woman' (p. 58) and two large mourning figures, which he did for an exhibition of monuments in 1909. Here, many of the characteristics of his first big sculpture of the Paris years, the 'Standing Woman' in marble (p. 61), are already discernible. Some small angels for the same exhibition, on the other hand, still tend too much toward the superficially decorative. Here the artist senses his ultimate goal but does not yet seem clearly conscious of it.

Of all the works of the Düsseldorf period one small figure stands out. This was a model made for a competition for a sculpture for the lobby of a commercial building. It is a standing figure (p. 56 left), marvelously concentrated in its contours. Of statuesque build, pure and noble in form, its slender lines hint at the work of his maturity.

'Man' (p. 56), a three-foot-high figure, was one of the last works of his Düsseldorf years. Lehmbruck understood that what matters is man in all his majesty and depth. This figure, done in 1909, seems to stride ahead though deep in thought, the head inclined, right arm thrown back over the head. It strikes one like a sculptural revelation of the artist's own brooding nature. The conception and form is somewhat Michelangelesque and the execution vaguely reminiscent of Rodin. It is a concentrated work, full of an inner tension that manifests itself in the arching of the muscular body into a powerful S-curve.

In his years of apprenticeship Lehmbruck was as deeply concerned with the intellectual basis as with the technique of his art. In hard work

18

he acquired the education which he had failed to get during his short years of formal schooling. The literary themes of his early sculptures and the etchings of his later years indicate that he incorporated what he had read into his work. In so doing he was concerned with the spirit of the literary work, not with illustration. Occasionally he also tried his hand at writing.

In looking at art both old and new, he wanted to know how the artist achieved his effects, and this is reflected in his etchings of an Egyptian sculpture in the Vatican, a Cimabue Madonna, and a Crucifixion after an Italian painting. His solitary, brooding mind shaped that which here offered itself to him.

In 1907 and 1908, Lehmbruck submitted to the Paris Salon his early 'Bather' (p. 52), 'Mother and Child' (p. 54), the 'Portrait Bust of the Painter W.' (p. 50), 'Road to Beauty' and 'Bust of a Lady.' He was accepted and to his immense satisfaction was made a member of the 'Société Nationale des Beaux-Arts.' Paris, which he visited for the first time in 1908, was the city of his dreams and he expected to find in it the inner freedom and inspiration he needed. In early 1910, he moved there.

Düsseldorf with its academically conventional art life had not allowed Lehmbruck to spread out and grow as much as he had wanted. But with great perseverance, moving ahead slowly, he had made everything he could learn there his own. His technical proficiency, the deep understanding of anatomy, the sure grasp of everything that could be seen, all these he acquired in serious work in the long years of his apprenticeship. It was there also that he solved the problem of which material best suited him. At first he worked in wood. But marble proved more to his liking, and he executed several works in marble: the 'Two Beggars,' the 'Head of a Girl,' tombstone reliefs, the bust of 'Count St.' Later he again worked in marble, sculpting the large standing woman now at the Duisburg Museum, a portrait bust of a woman,

19

a female torso, and the 'Bust of Mrs. L.' But he was not one of those sculptors who extracts the hidden elements of a block of stone or a stump of wood. Rather he was the born sculptor who sensitively feels the gentlest movement and who invests the modeling clay with animated movement. He therefore cast his figures in cement or in bronze, the material he preferred above all others.

Lehmbruck the Rhinelander with the innate Classicism was attracted by the refinement and self-assured traditionalism of Paris. He felt at home there, and he was able to compete with the creative forces of his time, to battle with them in a happy give-and-take. He was one of the most highly thought-of German artists in Paris. In the artistic atmosphere of Paris he was able to shed many of his inhibitions and discover his own, highly personal mission. Creative powers which had lain dormant far too long began to break through with elemental force.

Composition. Oil, 1913

Missing (formerly in the National Gallery, Berlin)

THE PARIS YEARS

Shortly after settling in Paris, Lehmbruck exhibited the final work of his Düsseldorf period, the colossal statue 'Man,' in the Salon de Printemps. Soon after, the standing figure of a woman was shown in the Salon d'Automne. A more profound change of style in so short a time is hardly to be imagined. The rough planes and some of the details of the 'Man' are reminiscent of Rodin, but in the figure of the woman, Lehmbruck's innate feeling for spatial values and disciplined structure suddenly emerged, and all that which slumbered like a seed in his early works suddenly unfolded. He now proclaimed the meaning of a work through form and proportion, whereas before he thought he had to express it in literary terms, in gesture and narrative. Ultimate peace is radiated by the stance of this marvelous sculpture, this woman endowed with infinite grace and classical beauty. This lovely figure pulsates with life. Sensuous fullness is paired with shy purity. Rarely has a German artist succeeded in presenting such a harmonious picture of physical nobility. One has to look at this figure from all angles to grasp the richness of structure, the silhouette, the gentle movement. Each aspect is wonderfully fulfilled. The rear view with its softly inclined head (p. 61) is a delightful revelation. The surface of this marble body, so alive and animated, is formed with incomparable sensitivity. The sculptural values may suffer somewhat in the marble version as compared to the cement and bronze; the smoothness and refinement of this stone are somewhat intrusive, but on the other hand, marble affords us a clearer view of the purity of structure and line. The face and the relaxed pose express a melancholy reverie and meditative withdrawal, foreshadowing the special qualities that were to mark the art of Wilhelm Lehmbruck.

Now the accumulated skill of a long apprenticeship began to bear rich fruit. Lehmbruck never lost his sure vision, not even in his most daringly exaggerated flights. Natural truth and true life remained part of his work. His gifted hands translated his innermost emotions into strong, expressive cultural values.

The statuette 'Girl Standing with Leg Propped' (pp. 66, 67) of his early Paris years is a work full of grace, harmonious in its lines and proportions. Here, too, warm life pulsates beneath the surface. The head is slightly inclined, thoughtfully leaning against the hands; the lines and curves are self-contained. Thus, despite the movement of the slightly protruding left knee, it is a cohesive entity.

The bust of Lehmbruck's wife (pp. 63, 64) has a monumental grandeur, with its softly expansive broad planes, as concentrated in expression as in form. It is a work of timeless scope and validity. The pictorial serves only as the incentive for the work, not as the goal.

By now Lehmbruck had achieved inner freedom. The artistic impulse continued to grow, the intention became clearer, the form more concentrated. The essence of the inner emotion became more penetratingly revealed in the form. Physical beauty, which Lehmbruck was able to present with such consummate mastery and sensitivity, began to recede in importance; as his figures took on a spiritual quality and everything superfluous was discarded it became a symbol. Everything focused on the essential. The 'Standing Woman' (1910) carries her head like a blossom on a stem. The dreamy, sad contemplation, the inward gaze, all this is here concentrated in the sculptural calm of the work, in its serene pose and line. The inner expression of the 'Young Contemplative Girl' (p. 73) is more brooding and pained. The folded arms and the garment wound around the legs arrest all movement, endowing the sculpture with great formal concentration. There no longer exists any externalized gesture; all movement is inner-directed. The head with its high forehead, its sad eyes and mouth, is tilted.

Next to these figures, the bronze relief 'Temptation' (p. 65), of which there exist also pen and watercolor sketches, at first strikes one as odd. The agitation of these figures is the antithesis of the statuary solidity of the earlier works. The sculptural technique here is also completely loose, far more so even than Rodin's. Everything is subordinated to the expressive movement, the flow of the line, the play of light and shadow. This movement and loosening of form is like a preparation, an acquisition of new freedom, for the great tasks lying ahead. It is typical of Lehmbruck that this group was done in relief rather than in full sculpture. It is the sort of work he usually did one-dimensionally, painting, drawing, and etching the movements of the bodies.

Only a year after that, his great 'Kneeling Woman' (pp. 74–81), the work which so boldly blazed the trail for new sculptural expression, and which proclaimed Lehmbruck's mission so clearly and logically, was exhibited in Paris. In retrospect it is difficult to appreciate what an incredible intellectual achievement this represented. Only with this work had he come into his own fully. All second-hand ideas and concepts of his years of learning were now definitely thrown off. At that period probably only George Minne, the noble, quiet Flemish sculptor, supported him in his new approach to a profoundly spiritualized sculpture. The fine, harmonious lines of Minne's drawings and etchings resemble spiritual sketches rather than physical descriptions. This downgrading of the physical in favor of emotion is deeply related to Lehmbruck's work. Yet Lehmbruck, younger and more robust, found a stronger and more personal way of stating that which he wanted to say.

Lehmbruck was of course acquainted with his contemporaries in Paris. Eduard Trier tells of Lehmbruck's contacts with Brancusi and Archipenko, with Modigliani and Matisse and Kogan. Undoubtedly

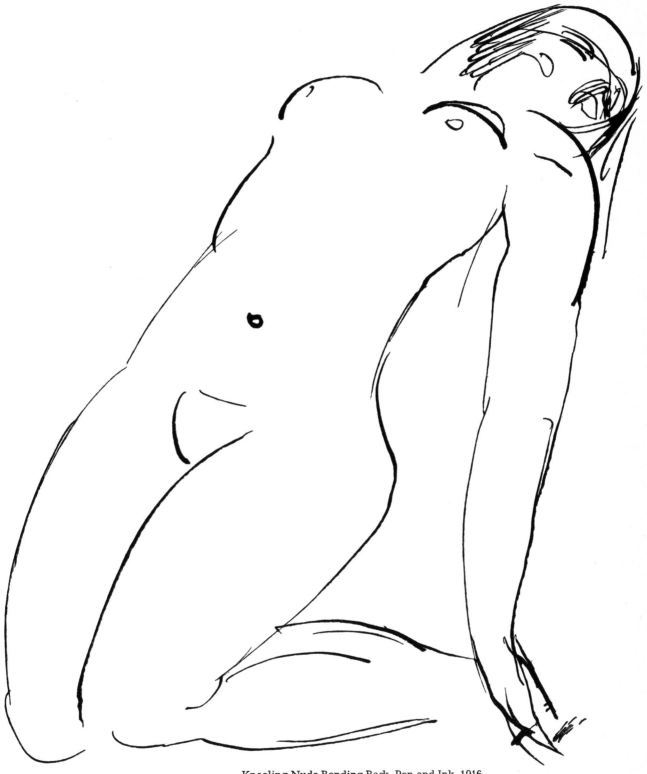

Kneeling Nude Bending Back. Pen and Ink, 1916

these artists confirmed Lehmbruck in his conviction that sculpture had to serve as an expression of the times.

What we find most moving even in these early products of his Paris years is their depth and tenderness, their intimacy and inwardness, that which was part of himself. But not until the 'Kneeling Woman' were these spiritual forces given pure expression, free from all outside influence. The head and gesture tell of an indescribable, moving depth of feeling which permeates every detail of the sculpture. The slender figure seems to be outside of everything physical, and yet it possesses an intimate naturalness. But it is a naturalness so pure and chaste that nothing detracts from its spirituality, humility, and contemplation, from its bowing down and submissiveness. This eloquent movement conveys a feeling of unbroken stillness devoid of all extraneous rhetoric. Full of joy, the figure listens inwardly as to far-off, mysterious voices. The eye looks inward, the head is gently inclined. The touching movement of the right hand points inward. All the curves are self-contained; no line leads to the outside. This slender figure is spiritualized, breaking away from the heaviness of the earth and yet remaining close to it in humility. Sensual appeal seems to have become a matter of indifference to this body. The medieval mystics must have possessed the characteristics embodied in this woman, the humble gaze looking inward, the devout waiting for the bestowing of spiritual grace.

With the 'Kneeling Woman,' Lehmbruck completed his spiritual breakthrough; inner content now became pre-eminent and created the bold means of expression according to its own laws. What mattered from here on was not aesthetic appeal and beauty of form. Still this attenuated figure retained a wonderful spiritual yet sensuous naturalness. The entire movement seems spread on a plane; the side view is strongly emphasized. Yet here, too, every angle is self-contained and highly expressive. The movement is not dramatic but full of gentle lyricism. The back curves gently and ends in the characteristically slender line from neck to head. The counterline of the bent knee and animated curve of the arms is substantially richer and more agitated. The left arm rests lightly on the knee, with open palm and as if in harmony with the melodic curve of the body. The marvelous movement of the right arm across the breast is very sensitive. The harmonization of this movement with the curves of the body is of great artistic and spiritual expressiveness. Despite the emphasized side view, one has to walk around this figure to fully appreciate its richness. There is not a superfluous line; the movement is continuous. This is a work of rare spiritual and formal unity and cohesion.

Lehmbruck also cast the head of the 'Kneeling Woman' separately (c.f. p. 78), for it expresses the essence of this work. This detail makes particularly tangible the unbelievably fluid line of the back to the stemlike neck and from the neck to the head. This long line, so characteristic of Lehmbruck, lands emphasis to the counterline of the face.

Two works which one would hardly expect to find alongside the 'Kneeling Woman,' because they are so close to nature also belong to the fruitful years 1910–11. They are two sculptures of the eldest of Lehmbruck's three sons. In them one can feel the happy father looking at his child. With charm and freshness, he has captured the clumsy crawling of the little boy in a small sculpture which he called a paperweight (p. 71). In another one the boy sits like a baroque Cupid (p. 70), one little leg pulled up, the other swinging over the edge of his perch. Of course these are minor works, but they afford us a glimpse into the soul of the artist, reflecting his love of nature and his great technical skill.

The bowing and incline of a slender woman's body, which is shaped so sensuously, coherently, and movingly into an expressive gesture in the 'Kneeling Woman,' is brought into pure, so-to-speak unintentional, sculptural movement in the 'Female Torso' (pp. 68–69). The angle of the body boldly spans space and ends in the long sweeping line of the head. The expression of the face is disarmingly shy.

The 'Ascendant Youth' (pp. 88–91) is the most moving of his Paris sculptures. The tragic seriousness of this young man seems like a reflection of Lembruck's own spiritual battles, like a highly personal document. The lean figure with the powerful legs haltingly strides upward to pure heights. His is not the rejoicing, liberated upward sweep of the sculptures found on the pillars of Gothic cathedrals. It is the trek of contemporary man, filled with anxious doubts and inhibitions, toward higher realms. The heroic beginning, the devout upward striving, are expressed in the energetic lines of the powerful limbs and the wiry strength of the torso. But the head is bent, marked by doubt and brooding, almost tired of the battle. With the upward motion of his right hand and index finger, the youth seems to point out and to confirm for himself the way up. But strong bonds keep him tied down, and these obstacles are expressed through the horizontal lines of the lower arms and shoulders. Thus the form itself carries on the tragic struggle of which the head offers such moving testimony. The upward line of the back, ending in the curve of the head, is particularly powerful. The energetic stride can best be appreciated from the side view with its bold movement of the left leg. This figure, unlike the sculptures of the early Gothic, stands free and unsupported; alone in space, it must fight its tragic battle. These truly grandiose and monumental sculptures remain lonely, without the joyous and liberating harmony of the architectural support afforded by medieval cathedrals. The subordination of the individual work to the totality of a structure was merely a symbol of the inner harmony of the church architecture of that age. Lehmbruck's times could not offer that. No architecture in harmony with his work was available to him. The work remained as lonely as its creator.

The disembodiment of the figure, its removal from the sphere of earthly beauty, its severity of form, all this is carried substantially further in the 'Ascendant Youth' than in the 'Kneeling Woman.' This young man dares to rise up out of misery and suffering to conquer pure, spiritual realms. The loose treatment of details, of feet, hands, and joints, contrasts sharply with the severity of the total form. Despite all his bold exaggeration, Lehmbruck remained natural in a higher sense, for he remained completely honest. If one wants to understand Lehmbruck, one must begin, as with all great art, with the forces that motivated him. Form and composition proclaim the human content of the figures; they express the convictions and emotions of their creator. Lehmbruck made art into a silent yet eloquent language of the soul.

The contemplation and longing, the reverie and sorrow of his early figures, were given mature and pure expression in his 'Large Contemplative Woman' (pp. 98–99), the fourth of the powerful, trail-blazing sculptures of his Paris period. One might call her the personification of contemplation. All physical weight has been lifted off this sublime figure. She is the expression of complete dedication. Her stillness is the personification of consummate silence. No sensuous beauty is allowed to distract us from her profound contemplation. The figure has an architectural quality. In the decisive vertical and horizontal structure, only the right leg is slightly out of line and the head gently inclined. The lines of the silhouette and the clear planes of the body emanate serenity and silence. Sharp and pure, growing away from everything earthly in its ascendant slenderness, this female body rests in itself. The joints are strong and the pivotal points emphasized. The left arm crosses on the back, and the hand grasps the loosely hanging right arm. This linking of the arms serves to underscore the majestic serenity. The completely spiritualized head on the slender neck is touching in the feeling of melancholy inwardness and contemplation which the entire work transmits. The strong body serves to emphasize the graceful proportion of the head. Of all the details of a figure which Lehmbruck also cast separately, the head gives the greatest feeling of being an entity in itself.

The formal discipline and simplicity of the body of this woman expressed Lehmbruck's ideas about proportions so perfectly that he made a version of only the torso from the knees up, without the arms (p. 117). This figure so pre-occupied him that he kept working on it until the end of his life. The marble sculpture still shows punctures and chisel marks; the completing touch still seems to be missing. This torso is the condensation of the total work. Its noble proportions, its classical purity, tell us as few other of his works do what Lehmbruck felt to be the essence of sculpture. His 'Standing Woman' was a step towards this ultimate spatial concentration, this closed entity.

The same concentration is also to be found in his 'Torso of a Girl' (p. 94) and in the more terse 'Torso of a Girl Turning Back' (p. 93). Despite its taut structure, the latter surges with life. Shyly modest, the girl looks back dreamily and with a sense of foreboding. This torso possesses even greater sculptural softness and richness than the 'Large Contemplative Woman' (p. 98). 'The Head of a Girl, Turning' (p. 72) is another example of the parts of a larger sculpture standing for the whole.

The spiritual reticence of woman permeates a model for 'Woman Looking Back' (p. 101), which was done before the 'Ascendant Youth' (p. 88). The sculptural form is tautly controlled; the sweep of movement is only hinted at. Because of its unfinished freshness this model has a mysterious and fascinating moving quality.

Lehmbruck's boldest exaggeration of proportion is to be found in the statuette 'Seated Girl' (p. 85). Here the silhouette has a broad sweep, its great curves describing an almost dancing movement. Within a small framework, Lehmbruck here goes far beyond the linear control of the monumental 'Kneeling Woman' (p. 74). Every movement here has its countermovement, all lines come back into themselves, making even so agitated a form as this self-contained. The head of this girl, brooding and bent, looks inward. The immediacy of every detail coupled with the refinement of the entire work, endows the exaggerations with realism.

In his bronze relief 'Three Women' (p. 103), Lehmbruck achieved a superb harmony of rhythmic placement of the slender figures in space. The relationship of the movements of the two standing figures and the sitting woman to one another and to the relief seems to symbolize a pure and serene existence amid their surroundings and at the same time a connection with a more spiritual world.

The freedom found in Lehmbruck's works after his arrival in Paris, a city which he loved and whose artistic atmosphere enriched his life, is particularly striking if one compares them to the works of his Düsseldorf period. There is almost no connection between his 'Bather' of 1905 and the sculpture of 1914 (p. 92). The former is a pleasant example of superb technique, while the latter is quietly concerned with itself, is complete in itself, mass and contour. Her movements veil rather than reveal. True, this woman is more physical than his other works of that period. The bold breaking-off at the calves emphasizes the forward thrust even more strongly. The line of the back, noble and unified, is counterbalanced by a more agitated treatment of the front view.

For the Werkbund Exhibition held in Cologne in 1914, Lehmbruck did two colossal figures, a man and a woman, which found an impressive setting on the ledges of an old fort. For the first and only time, Lehmbruck had the good fortune to have his works given a permanent place in harmony with the surroundings. An artist able to endow his works with such monumentality wants to see them well-housed. Proper placement of his works, not only while they are on exhibition, is the aspiration of every sculptor. Here in Cologne, Lehmbruck placed the two figures in the protective setting of the park, in true harmony with his conception. But because the war broke out shortly after the exhibition opened, we do not have any photographs of the sculptures 'in situ.' And because Lehmbruck did not have the means to have them crated and stored, these cement casts deteriorated. There was a cast of the powerful 'Standing Man' (p. 87 left) in Paris, which for a time was on loan to the museum at Duisburg, but this was destroyed in 1940. This sinewy figure stood carelessly leaning against a support which formed a strong vertical line with the torso. Confident and serene, it is a picture of man lost in thought and contemplation.

Man Looking Out. Chalk

Bather. Oil, 1913. Duisburg

BERLIN

When the war broke out, Lehmbruck hurriedly left Paris with his family. It may be assumed that much was lost in this move. He settled in Berlin, and in the first year there he completed the final version of 'Woman Looking Back' (p. 101), for which he had made a model in Paris. In this sculpture, the backward movement of the head is shy and gentle, the body cohesive. It is a sculpture of powerful spatial feeling. From whatever angle one looks at it, the contours of the figure form a softly moving curve.

Lehmbruck's portraits are evidence of his own rich inner life, for every good portrait is marked by the spirit of its creator. The profound humanity of Lehmbruck was already reflected in the heads of his Düsseldorf period, as for example in the 'Portrait Bust of the Painter W.' (p. 50), or in the noble gentleness of 'Count St.' All the heads of large figures which he cast separately tell of the doleful introspection and brooding depth of their creator. The image of man which Lehmbruck saw with his inner eye here takes on a visionary quality. The furrowed head of an old lady was apparently done at the time of the 'Ascendant Youth' (1913). But Lehmbruck did his most mature and most telling portraits during his Berlin and Zürich years. Despite all their realism and likeness, these nonetheless reveal uncommonly much of the artist's personality and attitude towards life. The 'Portrait Busts of Mr. and Mrs. F.' (p. 104 left and middle) transmit a feeling of security and serenity. The lines and finely-curved planes flow simply and majestically, particularly in the marble bust of 'Mrs. F.' Portraits of this type might be called monuments of human and personal traits.

34

For the 'Portrait Bust of Mrs. F.,' for which Lehmbruck made a plaquette, drawings, etchings, and a lithograph, he also did a remarkable statuette (p. 107). The gown of harmonious grace in which this figure is dressed makes the work into a highly concentrated sculptural entity and gives it strong contours and rhythm. It is the only clothed figure done by the later Lehmbruck.

The painful reverie and melancholic contemplation which mark so many of Lehmbruck's works are also etched into the lines of the eyes, temples, nose, and mouth of the 'Portrait Bust of Mrs. Oeltjen' (p. 105 left). The fragment of the life-size 'Bust of Miss K.' (p. 120) shows a similarly powerful expressiveness. The portrait bust of the poet Theodor Däubler, of which there also exist a lithograph and drawings, remained unfinished.

The war years weighed down heavily on the sensitive Lehmbruck. He invested a number of moving, important works with all the suffering of mankind. The vision of the 'Fallen Warrior' (p. 111) is like a premonition of the tragic fate which was to befall his country and his people. The broken sword the warrior holds in his tired right hand is useless; he falls, mortally wounded, even though he rebels against his fate with his head, his legs, and his upper arms. It is a fall starkly rendered by the artist. The sudden downward slant of the line of the back and the nape of the neck commands attention and convinces us of the inevitability of his fate. The arched arms and thighs are like structures cast in concrete. The mortally wounded warrior is rebelling against his downfall until the very last. But this desperate struggle against the power of death turned against man is in vain. The strong, pitiless formation of the body makes for an unusually moving symbol of the heroic battle of the mortally wounded warrior.

Lehmbruck depicted the war only symbolically, not in pictorial episodes. His 'Attacker' (p. 108) is a fascinating, emotional statuette. Excitement animates not only its gesture, it vibrates throughout the entire body, whose rich surface shimmeringly reflects the light. But the warrior seems to be hit just as he is storming ahead; he is in the process of lowering his left arm and his body bends back as if about to fall.

THE LAST YEARS IN ZÜRICH AND BERLIN

Even though Lehmbruck moved to peaceful Switzerland in 1917 and opened a studio in Zürich, he continued to grieve over the misery brought on by the war. His most moving plaint, and at the same time his last monumental work, is the 'Seated Youth' (p. 119). He originally intended to name the figure 'The Friend.' Many of Lehmbruck's friends on both sides had died in this catastrophic war. The youth sitting here is mourning them and all the other dead. Nothing is allowed to soften the bitter pain; no physical beauty distracts the viewer. Completely engulfed in his grief, the youth sits bent over. The sculptural expression is stern and true. The structure is sparse and we are able to share the young man's sense of loss. Nothing in the world seems to concern him any longer. He is completely alone with his sorrow and anguish.

This sculpture was later erected in the soldiers' cemetery of Lehmbruck's native city. There he sits on a low pedestal in the middle of a broad lawn. A tree spreads its branches overhead, imparting a feeling of solitude and space, a serenity and seclusion in keeping with the inner meaning of the work.

A 'Female Torso' fragment (p. 116) made in his Zürich years seems to stretch its arms heavenward, as if in entreaty. Here everything is only hinted at and hence full of mystery. The body, the arms, and the neck lean toward the right with strong emphasis, a gesture tantamount to a moving outcry.

The 'Bust of Fritz von Unruh,' also a product of his Zürich years, embodies Lehmbruck's idea of what a poet should look like. At about that time he also made two versions of the 'Portrait Bust of Mrs. B.' (p. 115), a marble version of the 'Head of Mrs. L.' which was never completed, and two sketchy portraits of Miss B. 'The Portrait Bust of Miss von Fr.' (p. 105 right), completed shortly before Lehmbruck's tragic death in Berlin, is filled with sorrowful melancholy.

Throughout his life, Lehmbruck was moved by the mysterious bond between mother and child. He did some mother and child studies while still in Düsseldorf, a theme which continued to preoccupy him in sculpture, drawing, and painting. One of his later works, 'Mother and Child' (p. 122), is a final and definitive treatment of this eternal theme. In his early sculptures, the deep ties between mother and child were represented more or less literally. In this late version, Lehmbruck with deep feeling offers a profound insight into this mystical bond. The mother, the soil from which new life springs, turns to the child with a gentle smile full of feeling and sadness. Her gaze is the essence of maternal concern. The child, sleeping and feeling completely sheltered, huddles close to the mother.

Lehmbruck's lonely, brooding personality is expressed most purely and movingly in the 'Head of a Thinker' (p. 121). This is not the portrait of a man once seen in a contemplative pose like Rodin's statue. Neither is it the portrait of a philosopher, of any one man specifically. Rather, it is the essence of brooding and thought, doubting and searching, the forbidden fruit from the tree of knowledge, because of which man is condemned to passivity. The arms are useless stumps. Only the hand is clenched in despair at the breast. Beneath the powerful skull of this thinker there is doubt. This work is a pained outcry against the intellectual enslavement of contemporary man. Lehmbruck fought this rationalized world, he wanted to create a realm of the spirit, of noble emotions and profound experience. And he himself suffered the anguish so movingly portrayed here.

Although only a few of Lehmbruck's drawings and etchings deal with religious themes, all of his works might be termed 'pre-religious,' for every one of his creations is searching for the link with the eternal source of life. The 'Praying Woman' (p. 125), his last large sculpture, is not an image of unquestioning, liberating belief. Her hand is raised in supplication, her gaze is turned inward, and her lips are parted as if about to speak. The structure of her lean body is as severe as Egyptian sculpture, particularly if looked at from the side.

Truth and love are the hallmark of Lehmbruck's work. All his figures are the product of this great love and filled with it. His 'Heads of Lovers' (p. 124) are a fitting finale. They lean against each other sadly, as if looking for a place in which to cry to their hearts' content.

PAINTINGS, DRAWINGS, AND ETCHINGS

Lehmbruck was a born sculptor. His hands created figures that filled space, and just as they absorbed space they also moved into a new spiritual realm. They proclaimed their spiritual beauty and profundity to the world. And when their creator worked with other materials and searched for other means of expression, he remained a sculptor. He used other, more malleable materials only to contain his overflowing inner vision.

He handled brush, pencil, and etching needle with rare skill, jotting down his ideas as they came to him, freely and animatedly, in a way he could not have done in the slower and more difficult medium of sculpture.

Lehmbruck had painted while still in Düsseldorf. The youthful technique and realism of his oil portrait of a young girl (p. 127) is reminiscent of the Leibl school. This probably is not the first nor only venture into oil painting of his apprenticeship years. The number of his paintings on canvas, wood, or board is not great, probably only around thirty. As a rule his pictures are formed sparingly, extremely light and loose in conception; the colors, applied in thin layers, tend towards the cold tones. They are used to illustrate the form rather than being assigned strong independent values. Using light blue contours, more rarely brown or ochre, the artist would jot down the outlines of the bodies with animated lines, continue to work on them, make notes on the picture, and then frequently stop working on them. Consequently, there are few actually finished works among his paintings. But it is precisely the creative freshness and the mystery of the

Pieta, Oil, 1916. Private Collection

incomplete which stimulate the imagination of the viewer.

When in Paris, Lehmbruck saw the large figures of Maillol, which suggest a happy contentment in the beautiful, pure, earthly existence. He also gained completely new insight into the problems which Marées had raised as a painter, and he tried to deal with them in his drawings. In his 'Frieze of Women' done in 1910 (p. 128), a large, airy drawing, he has brought the rhythm of the entire picture, the organization of the standing and sitting figures, the horizontal and vertical tendencies, into a joyous harmony. The movements of the figures are taken up and carried further by a few background lines, which makes for a well-defined linear structure. The figures in their ideal world stand secure and protected. The sensitive ease of line and the animation of the stroke enhance the innate joy of their ideal condition. The 'Three Women' (1910, p. 129) shows a similar harmony of line and rhythmic balance. In 1915 he again dealt with the theme of three women, but here his standing and sitting figures are much freer in composition, more concentrated in their proportions, more profound in their utilization of space, and far more expressive. With the help of a few spots of color in the background, Lehmbruck achieved a unique feeling of depth and space without resorting to perspective. This lends the picture an oddly spiritual profundity.

Most of Lehmbruck's compositions are filled with a gentle lyricism. In his early Paris years he was close to George Minne, and his 'Pilgrim' (p. 136), a kneeling figure jotted down on canvas with light blue contours, is vaguely reminiscent of Minne's lovely linear technique. Later, Lehmbruck's paintings and sculptures became more and more spiritualized. Figures such as 'Martha' (1912, p. 17) seem to come forth from mysterious depths, gently like dreams. Frequently there are only a few lines, the curve of a body, a head, hints which Lehmbruck jots down on canvas; but they affect us and grow into a meaningful entity. His drawings are unusually persuasive. Supremely sure of himself, Lehmbruck was able to come to grips with the great masters of the past and of his own time without running the danger of losing his way. That he was also influenced by Munch's demonic vision can be seen in the half nude of 1915 (p. 131), with the almost forbidding dark tones of the hair and background, and the half-closed, watchful eyes. Dark and heavy as none of his other pictures is a "Pietà" of 1916 (p. 41); deep-red and eerie white tones break through the black-gray. But the gentle, fervent visions predominate in his work, and Lehmbruck traces them with animated lines and gentle colors. The 'Bather' of 1913 (p. 33) is particularly lovely. With a minimum of means, a few lines and spots of brown, nothing more, Lehmbruck has given a woman's head done in 1914 (p. 134) a wealth of gentleness and emotion. Contemplative heads and figures predominate in his paintings as in his sculptures.

His paintings, unlike his sculptures, include dramatic scenes, such as 'Charon in Love' (p. 130), the big composition 'Inundation' (146 left), an 'Abduction' and the predominantly red 'Adam and Eve' and 'Flight,' both painted on two old door panels. The composition 'Bathsheba' (p. 132) is particularly mature and rich, with its powerful blue, its glowing red undertones, and its touches of ochre and yellow. Lehmbruck put down in his pictures that which he was unable to capture in his sculptures—the movement and countermovement of groups of people and their inner and outer conflict.

Lehmbruck's road from the concept to the completion of a sculpture was long. He worked, polished, and shaped each piece for a long time and would let it out of his studio only reluctantly, and he would resume work on already finished figures if he felt that he could bring new and more profound insights to them. This was not due to a lack of imagination and vision, but rather it was the result of a concern over what was valid and lasting. How rich his intuition was, how great his inspiration, is attested to by his drawings, notes, and sketches, of which more than six hundred have been preserved. Most of them are nothing

43

more than working drawings for his sculptures, compositional trials and preliminary sketches. Yet they tell us how he let an idea ripen, how he concentrated on it to achieve a sparser and more compelling expression, greater cohesion and organization. They offer us a glimpse into his method of work. The sketches that have been preserved show how rich was Lehmbruck's conception of gesture and line, of composition and spatial movement.

Most of the drawings, however, are personal notations of inner visions. He did not do the sort of polished, saleable drawing which is so common today. He worked on them only until he had retained what was in his mind's eye. But that is precisely why they are so effective, fresh, and persuasive. His watercolors and india ink drawings have the same gentle tones and convey the same spiritual feeling as his paintings. His gentleness and emotional restraint led him to the use of pastels. However, when he had a sudden idea, he usually drew, in order to retain the elusive image. In these drawings his lines are gossamer, an embodiment of the gentlest feelings. Apparently in doing them he was not concerned with beauty and lasting values: as a result his masterful skill is even more evident.

Lehmbruck began to etch and lithograph because of the same desire to retain a fleeting image in a graphic yet easily executed form. The delicacy of etching must have been particularly appealing to him. He liked to work with the cold needle, etching the surface and correcting as he went along. Thus in many of his etchings we can follow his progress as he clarified the composition. In the various stages of the plate Lehmbruck would continue to simplify the line, build it more definitely into the surface, strengthening the expressiveness of the physical movements. Often he would paint or draw over the finished etching. Being a sculptor, he had a sure feeling for what could be done with the surface. Here, too, he worked with only a few lines which sensitively divided a picture rhythmically.

The movements and countermovements of his figures only rarely tell a dramatic story. Even in his Shakespearean figures he depicts psychological situations. A gentle lyricism flows through the fine lines of these works, whose content, as in the sculptures, lies in the bowing and bending, the stride and the stance, the kneeling and the repose of a figure. Seldom did he do literary themes from the Bible or Dante or Shakespeare.

He placed the figures of his graphics as those of his paintings against the background with a few rough lines and shaped them with a few dark, strong contours. Because of its lyrical softness he preferred zinc to copper. Now and then graphic sketches accompany his sculptures, as in the 'Ascendant Youth,' 'Kneeling Woman' (p. 75), and some of the portraits busts. But here the function of the drawings is to retain an elusive image. They are not preliminary work sketches; they have an independent value and function. There are other drawings, nearly one hundred and fifty, which deal with the laws of composition of ancient sculptures and paintings.

In his approximately fifteen lithographs, Lehmbruck reverted to the themes of some of his sculptures, e.g., a portrait of Theodor Däubler (p. 143 right), the head of 'Mrs. F.' But these works also have their own life, and the means are used sparingly—a few easy, fluid lines suffice, because the concept and inner meaning are clear.

The graphic works and the many drawings are a painful reminder of how many great and rare sculptures still remained to be done when Lehmbruck died. His work had certainly not been completed. He took his life on March 25, 1919, not because he had failed as an artist or because he had suffered a loss of inspiration and creativity but because he sought to escape from physical and psychic pain which his sick body was no longer able to bear. He went at the moment when success was assured. The Berlin Academy had just made him a member. Teaching posts were waiting for him. Appreciation of his art was spreading. The years of sacrifice had come to an end. But it was too late.

Lehmbruck's lifework was the torso. He himself has given us many versions of this symbol of non-completion. We are made painfully aware of the inadequacy of human existence in the face of the tragedy of so gifted and towering an artist. But his work, his spirit, his power and his depth, his greatness and his gentleness, live on.

The human values which are part of his sculptures have become rare in modern art. Today problems of pure form are in the limelight. Paul Westheim posed the question of who might be considered Lehmbruck's heir and has suggested Gerhard Marcks. Eduard Trier mentioned Robert Couturier. Lehmbruck did not apparently directly influence his contemporaries or younger sculptors, even though they have voiced their admiration of him. His art is rooted in a personal commitment, and therefore we may not be able to appoint an heir.

Lehmbruck's work and influence transcend the borders of Germany. He has been hailed and exhibited in many countries of the world—in the United States as well as in Europe.

LEHMBRUCK ON SCULPTURE

'I believe that we are once more moving toward a truly great art and that we will soon find the expression of our time in a monumental, appropriate, contemporary style. This art must be contemporary, not a revival of old styles, for never has good art grown out of the revival of styles of the past; it must be monumental, heroic, like the spirit of our age.

'Sculpture like all art is the highest expression of its age.

'Every work of art must have something of the first days of creation, of the smell of the earth, one might say something animal-like. All art is measure. Measure against measure, that is all. The measures or, in the case of figures, the proportions, determine the impression, the effect, the physical expression, the line, the silhouette—everything. Therefore a good sculpture must be handled like a good composition, like a building, where measure against measure matters; therefore one also cannot rule out the detail, for the detail is the gauge of the whole. The painter who divides the surface does the same thing as the sculptor who sees the volume of his statue as surface and divides it.

'Thus there exists no monumental, architectural art without outline or without silhouette, and silhouette is nothing but surface.

'I find this general feeling among some young artists from various countries, even though their works appear very different, and this feeling will guide them to a new contemporary expression, to the style of our day.

'Sculpture is the essence of things, the essence of nature, that which is eternally human.'

47

51

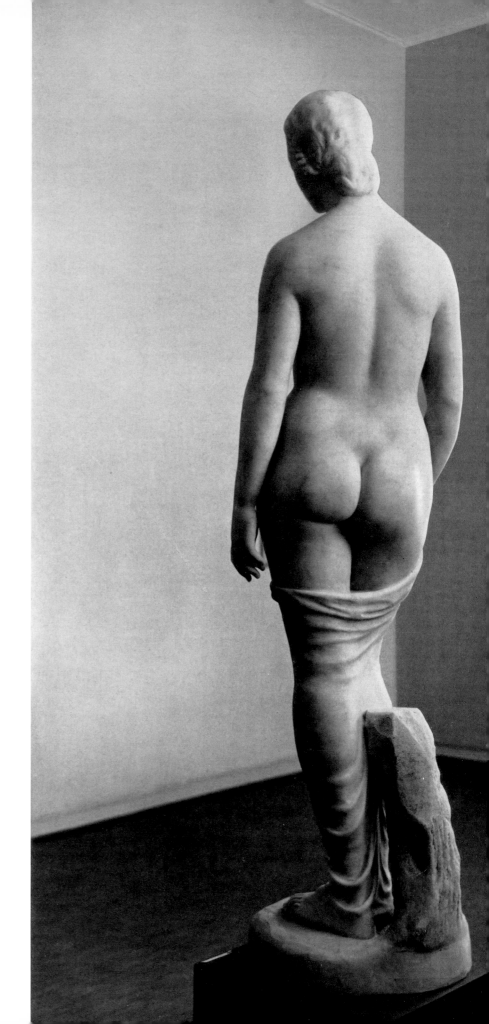

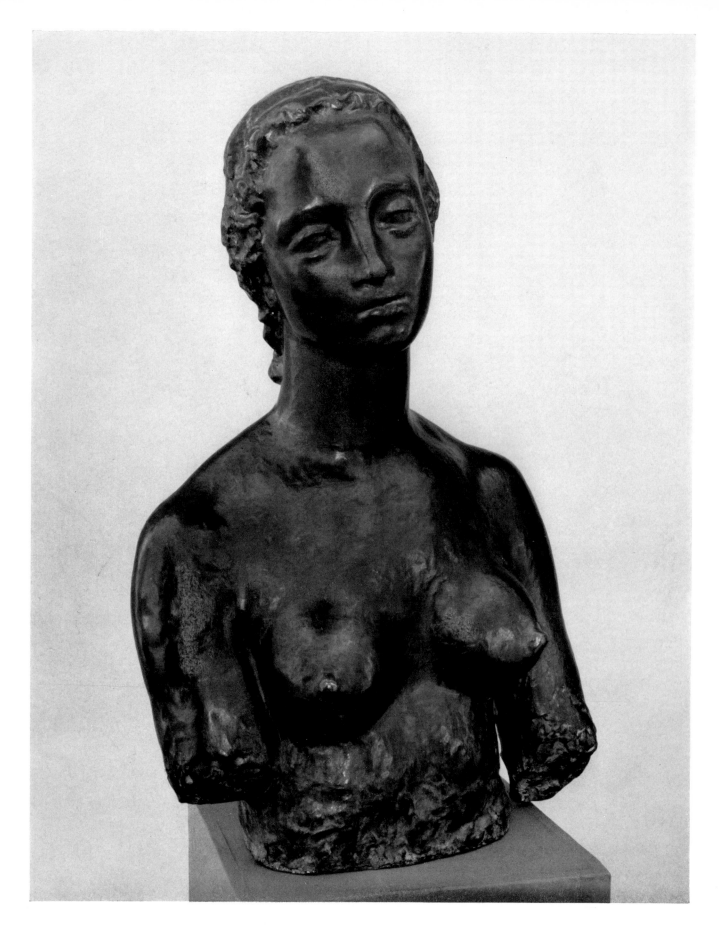

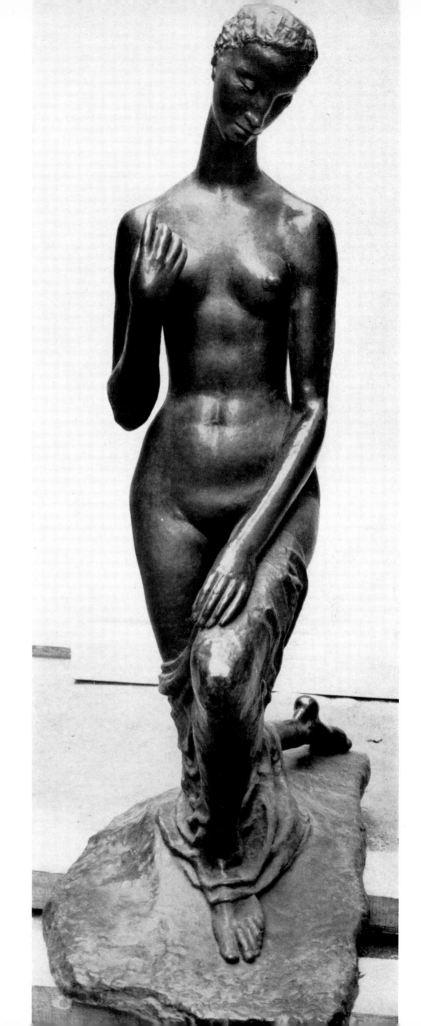

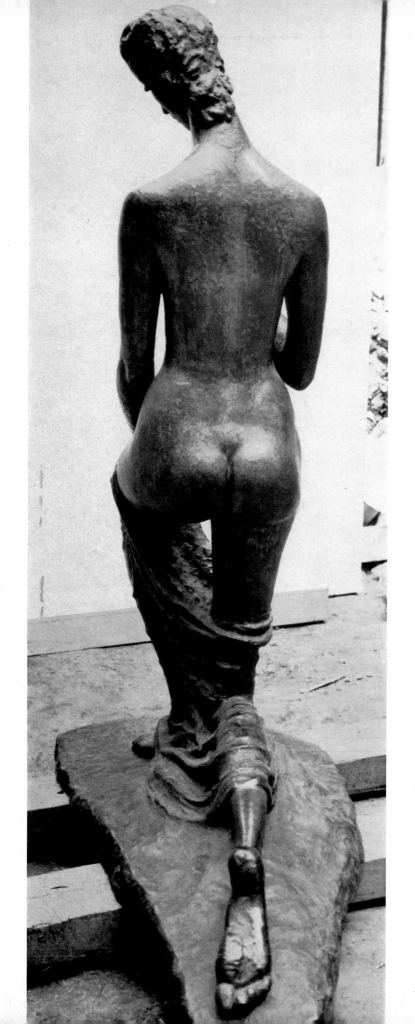

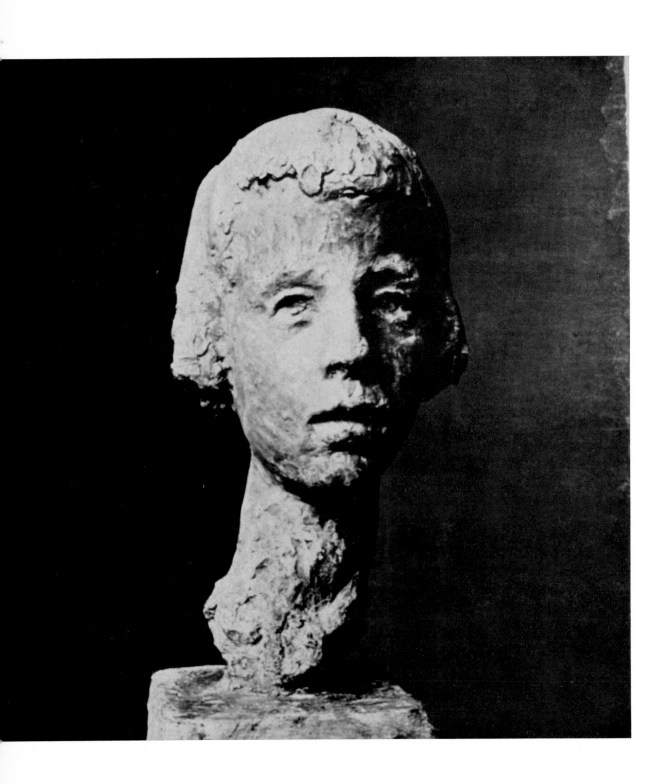

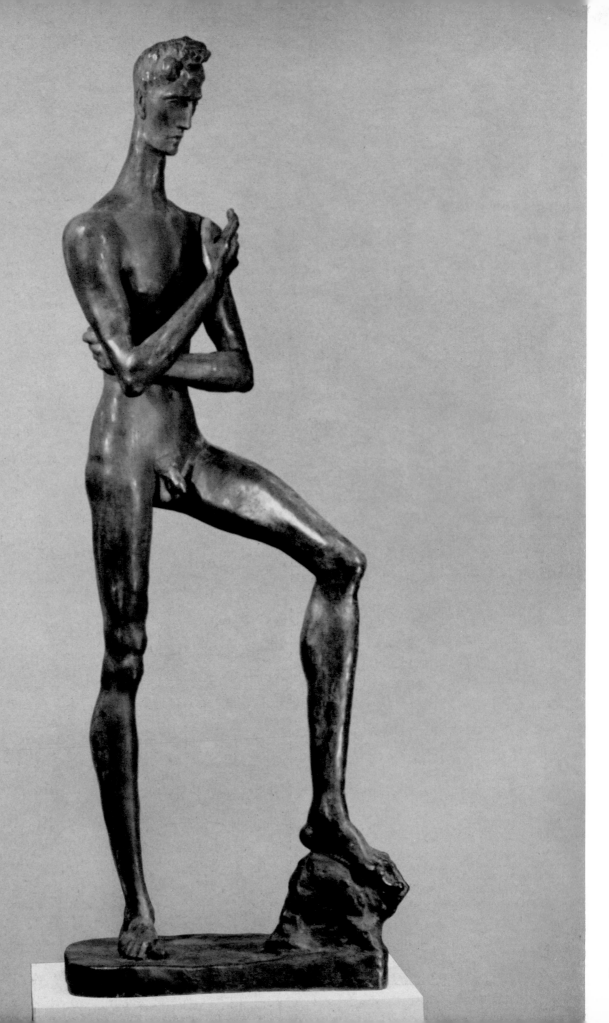

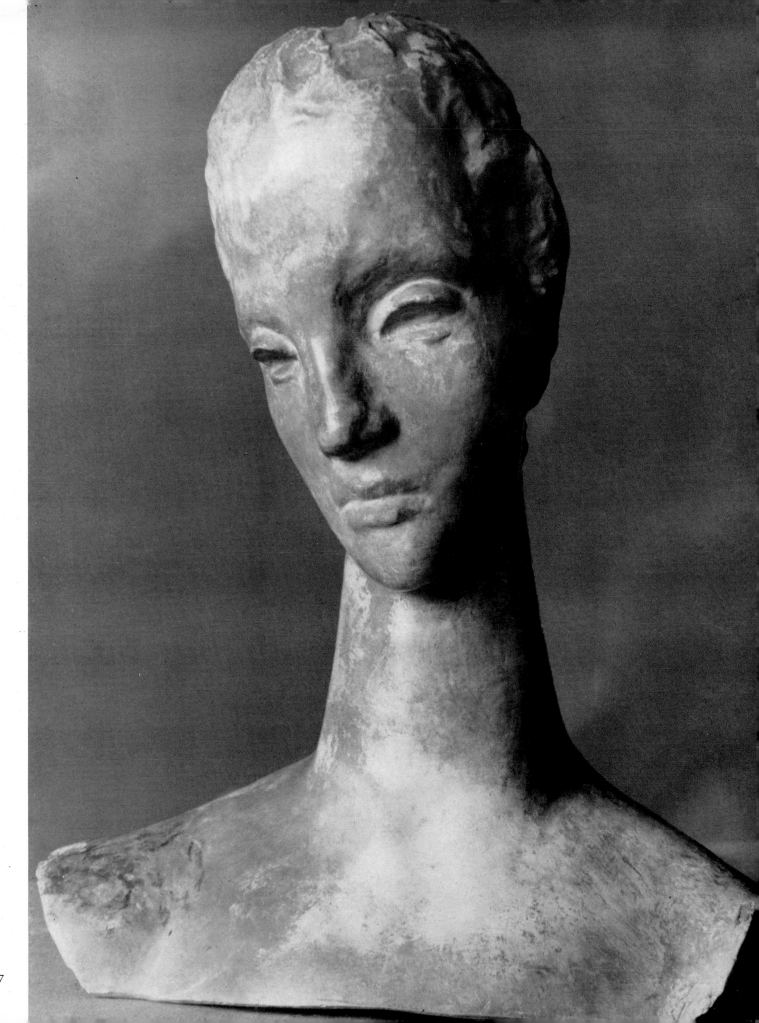

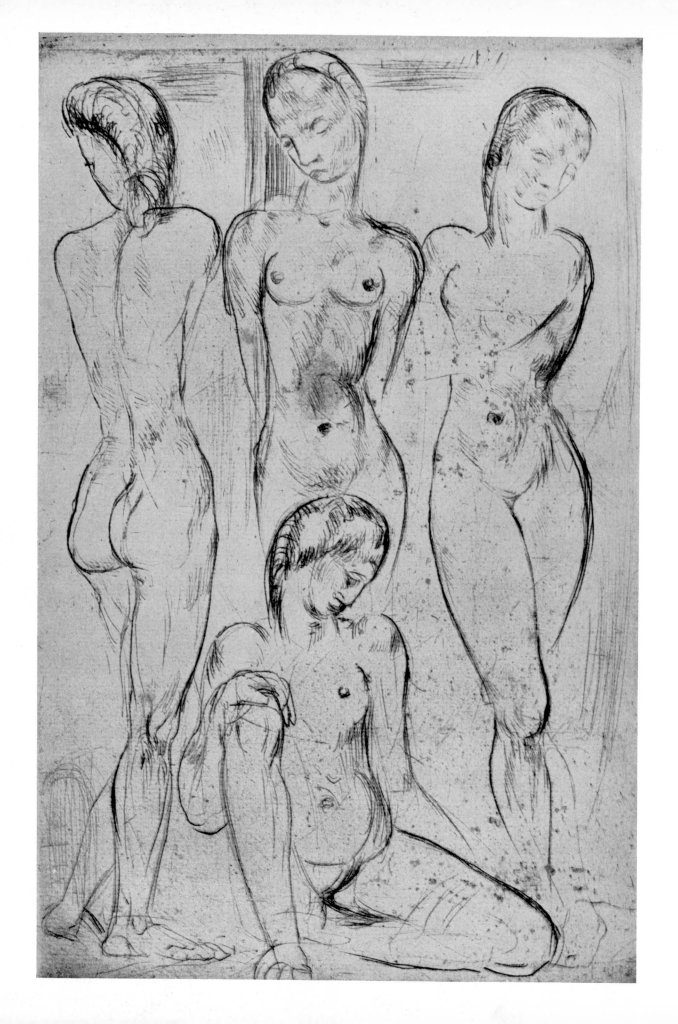

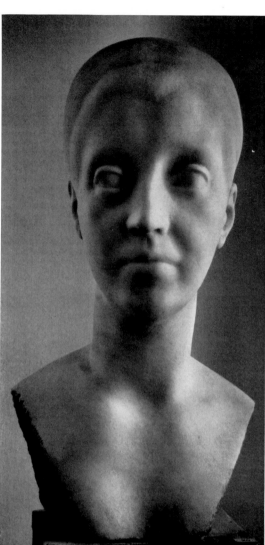

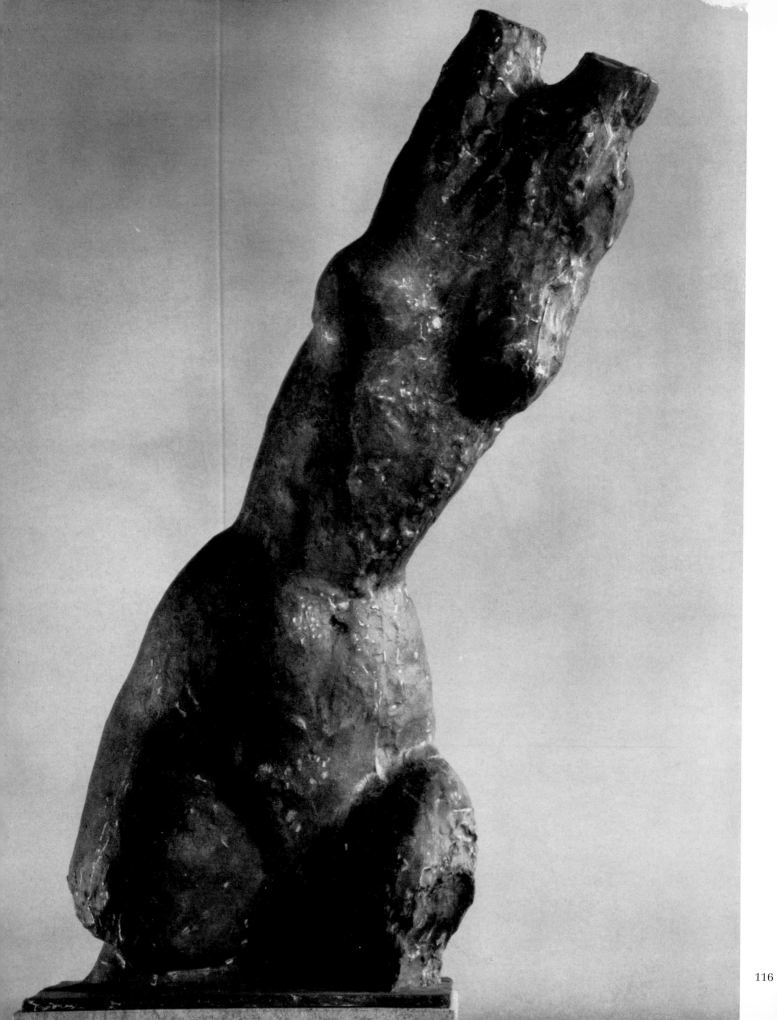

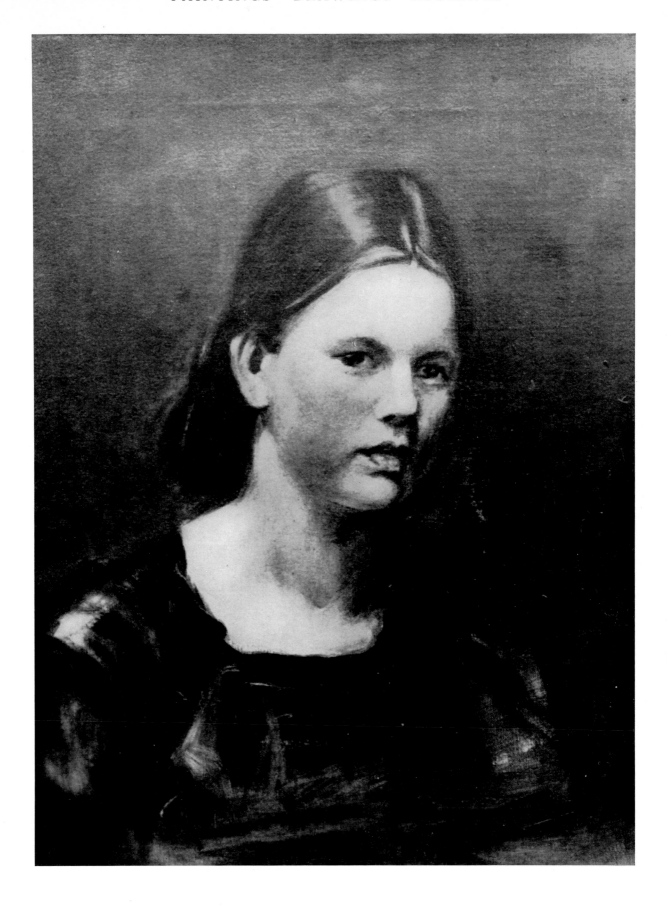

Orpheus
Eurydike

W. Lehmbruck
1913

135

Wilhelm Lehmbruck, 1903. Portrait by H. Wettig

Lehmbruck's birthplace in Duisburg

Wilhelm Lehmbruck
and his older brother

Wilhelm Lehmbruck at the age of sixteen

Lehmbruck and his wife in the studio in Düsseldorf

In the
studio in
Zürich

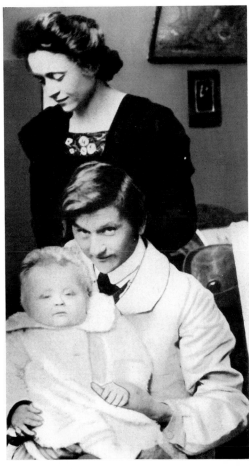

Lehmbruck with his wife and eldest son

Wilhelm Lehmbruck 1915

BIOGRAPHICAL DETAILS

1881.	Born on January 4th in Duisburg.
1895–99.	Attended a School of Applied Arts in Düsseldorf.
1899–1901.	Apprentice in a sculptor's studio in Düsseldorf.
1901–8.	Studied at Düsseldorf Academy of Art. Prize pupil of Karl Janssen.
1905.	First journey to Italy.
1907.	First exhibited in the Salon of the *Société Nationale des Beaux-Arts* in Paris. Met Rodin and Maillol.
1910–14.	In Paris. Studio and lodgings in Rue de Vaugirard. Meetings with Matisse and others of his school, with Archipenko, Brancusi, Modigliani, Derain, Le Fauconnier, Dunoyer de Segonzac and others.
1912.	Second journey to Italy.
1914–17.	In Berlin.
1917–18.	In Zürich.
1919.	Again in Berlin. Became member of the Prussian Academy of Arts. Committed suicide on March 25th.

Wilhelm Lehmbruck, 1916/17

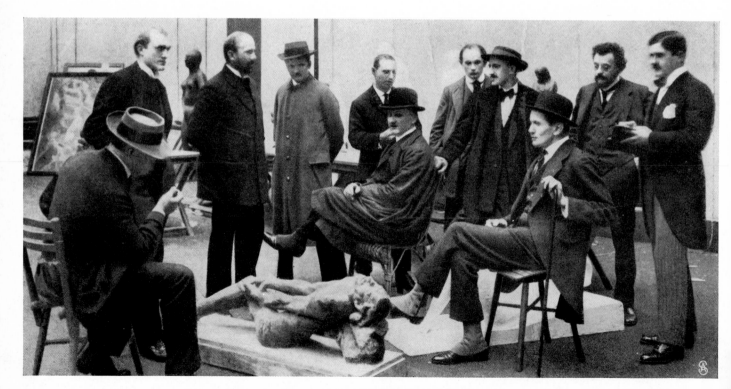

Jury session at the Free Secession.
From left to right: Prof. August Kraus, Max Beckmann, Walter Rösler, Wilhelm Lehmbruck, Benno Berneis, Konrad v. Kardorff, Erich Heckel, Walter Bondy, Prof. E. R. Weiß (seated), Ernst Barlach, E. Schall.

List of Plates

LIST OF PLATES

Frontispiece: Self-Portrait, 1902, black chalk

Text illustrations

8   Tired Warrior, pen and ink
11 The Fallen, charcoal
17 Martha, 1912, oil,
    Duisburg Municipal Art Collection
21 Composition, 1913, oil, missing
    (formerly in the National Gallery,
    Berlin)
25 Kneeling Nude Bending Back, 1916,
    pen and ink
32 Man Looking Out, 1914, chalk, Paris
33 Bather, 1913, oil,
    Duisburg Municipal Art Collection
41 Pietà, 1916, oil, privately owned

Plate Section

49 Woman's Head, 1910, bronze
50 Portrait Bust of the Painter W., 1906,
    Duisburg Municipal Art Collection
51 Miner, 1905, bronze relief,
    Folkwang Museum, Essen
52 Bather, 1905, bronze,
    Duisburg Municipal Art Collection
53 Bather, detail
54 Mother and Child, 1907, bronze,
    Folkwang Museum, Essen
55 Mother and Child, detail
56 l Female Figure, 1908, bronze,
    Duisburg Municipal Art Collection
56 r Man, 1909, plaster

57 Lost in Thought (Mother and Child),
    1907, bronze relief, Folkwang Museum,
    Essen
58 Sorrowing Woman, 1909, bronze relief,
    Duisburg Municipal Art Collection
59 Standing Woman, 1910, bronze,
    Folkwang Museum, Essen
60 Standing Woman, detail
61 Standing Woman, marble,
    Duisburg Municipal Art Collection
62 Torso of Standing Woman, cement
63 Head of Mrs. L., 1910, bronze
64 Bust of Mrs. L., 1910, bronze,
    Duisburg Municipal Art Collection
65 Temptation, 1911, bronze relief,
    Duisburg Municipal Art Collection
66 Girl Standing with Leg Propped, 1910,
    bronze, Duisburg Municipal Art
    Collection
67 Girl Standing with Leg Propped, detail
68 Female Torso, 1910–11, cement,
    Folkwang Museum, Essen
69 Female Torso
70 Seated Boy, 1910, cement,
    Duisburg Municipal Art Collection
71 Child Crawling, 1910, bronze,
    Duisburg Municipal Art Collection
72 Head of a Girl, Turning, 1913–14,
    bronze
73 Young Contemplative Girl, 1911, bronze,
    Duisburg Municipal Art Collection
74 Kneeling Woman, 1911, bronze,
    Duisburg Municipal Art Collection
75 Pencil Sketch for Kneeling Woman, 1911
76 Kneeling Woman, detail

158

77   Kneeling Woman, front view

78   Kneeling Woman, detail

79   Kneeling Woman, detail

80   Kneeling Woman, rear view

81   Kneeling Woman, detail

82   Portrait of a Woman, crayon on linen, 1915

83   Woman's Head, 1911, bronze

84   Head of a Youth, 1912, cement

85   Seated Girl, statuette, 1913–14, cement

86   Female Torso, 1913, bronze

87 l Standing Man, 1914, cement, destroyed

87 r Model for Woman Looking Back, 1913, cement

88   Ascendant Youth, 1913, bronze

89   Ascendant Youth, detail

90   Head of Ascendant Youth

91   Ascendant Youth

92 l The Bather, 1914, bronze

92 r The Bather, 1914, cement

93   Torso of Girl Turning Back, 1913–14, bronze

94   Torso of Girl, 1913–14, cement

95   Torso of Girl, 1913–14, cement (after sustaining war damage)

96   Girl's Head on Slender Neck, 1913–14, cement

97   Girl's Head on Slender Neck, 1913–14, cement

98   Large Contemplative Woman, 1913–14, bronze

99   Large Contemplative Woman, rear view

100   Head of Girl, 1913–14, terracotta

101   Woman Looking Back, 1914–15, bronze

102   Four Women, 1913, etching

103   Three Women, 1914, bronze relief

104 l Portrait Bust of Mr. F., 1915–16, bronze

104 m Portrait Bust of Mrs. F., 1915–16, marble, Duisburg Municipal Art Collection

104 r Woman's Head, cement

105 l Portrait Bust of Mrs. Oeltjen, 1915–16, cement

105 r Portrait Bust of Miss von Fr., 1919, cement

106   Portrait Mask of Mr. F., 1915–16, cement

107   Portrait Statuette of Mrs. F., 1015–16, terracotta, Staedel Museum, Frankfurt

108   The Attacker, 1914–15, bronze statuette

109   Two Stricken Young Attackers, 1916–17, lithograph

110   The Fallen Warrior, 1915, chalk

111   The Fallen Warrior, 1915–16, cement

112   The Fallen Warrior, detail

113   The Fallen Warrior, 1915, charcoal

114   The Fallen Warrior, detail

115   Portrait Bust of Mrs. B., 1918, cement

116   Female Torso, fragment, 1918, bronze, Duisburg Municipal Art Collection

117   Female Torso, 1918, marble (destroyed)

118   Seated Youth, detail, 1918, bronze, Duisburg Municipal Art Collection

119   Seated Youth

120   Bust of Miss K., fragment, 1916, cement

121   Head of a Thinker, 1918, bronze

122   Mother and Child, 1917–18, bronze, Duisburg Municipal Art Collection

123   Mother and Child, 1917–18, cement

124   Heads of Lovers, 1918, cement

125   Praying Woman, fragment, 1918, cement

127   Head of a Girl, 1906, oil

128   Frieze of Women, 1910, crayon

129   Three Women, 1910, oil (destroyed, formerly Kaiser-Friedrich-Museum, Magdeburg)

159

130   Charon in Love, 1913, oil

131   Female Half Nude, 1915, oil

132   Bathsheba, 1913, oil

133   Portrait Study, 1914, oil

134   Woman's Head, 1914, oil

135   Orpheus and Eurydice, 1913,
       coloured pen drawing

136   The Pilgrim, 1911, crayon

137   Woman's Head, 1911, red chalk

138   Female Nude, 1912, pencil

139   Awakening Warrior, 1916, chalk

140   Woman's Head, black chalk,
       30.5 × 44 cm., signed W. Lehmbruck
       in right hand lower corner

141   Nude Reading, pencil, 16.5 × 25.2 cm.,
       not signed

142 l Seated Japanese Woman, 1916–17,
       lithograph

142 r Boy's Head, Turned Left, 1916–17,
       lithograph

143 l Mother and Child I, 1916–17,
       lithograph

143 r Portrait of Theodor Däubler, 1916–17,
       lithograph

144   The Oppressed, 1912, etching

145   Great Resurrection, 1913, etching

146 l Inundation, 1915, etching

146 r Shakespeare Visions, Macbeth II, 1918,
       etching

147 l Large Woman's Head, 1912, etching

147 r Paolo and Francesca, 1913, etching

148   The Prodigal Son, 1912, etching

149   Mother and Child, 1910, etching

150   Kneeling Woman, 1911, etching

151   Ascendant Youth, 1912, etching

Lehmbruck's life

153   Wilhelm Lehmbruck, 1903.
       Portrait by H. Wettig

154   Lehmbruck's Birthplace in Duisburg

154   Wilhelm Lehmbruck
       and his older brother

154   Wilhelm Lehmbruck
       at the age of sixteen

154   Lehmbruck and his wife
       in the studio in Düsseldorf

155   In the studio in Zürich, 1918

155   Lehmbruck with his wife and eldest son
       in Paris

155   Wilhelm Lehmbruck, 1915

156   Wilhelm Lehmbruck, 1916/17

156   Jury session at the Free Secession

ACKNOWLEDGMENTS

The plates are reproduced from photographs from the following sources:—

Archiv, Duisburg. Dräyer, Zürich. Epha, Duisburg. Folkwang Museum, Essen. Gnilka, Berlin. Hesse, Duisburg. Hoepffner, Hamburg. Kleinhempel, Hamburg. De Maeyer, Antwerp. Foto Marburg. Moegle, Stuttgart. Reclam, Renger. Salchow, Cologne. Sayers, London. Wagner, Hanover. Weishaupt, Stuttgart. Wölbing, Bielefeld.